today, tomorrow & every day

WRITTEN BY M.H. CLARK

DESIGNED BY JILL LABIENIEC

One day, she stepped back
and took a look at her life.

A LONG, CLOSE LOOK. AS THOUGH IT WERE A CITY
SHE LOVED AND SHE WAS FLYING HIGH ABOVE IT, SO
HIGH THAT SHE COULD SEE THE WHOLE THING.

*And she realized
something:*

SHE LIKED
WHAT SHE SAW.

———

SHE LIKED WHERE
SHE HAD BEEN.

———

SHE LIKED WHERE
SHE WAS GOING.

She hadn't always been this way.

SHE HADN'T ALWAYS BEEN AS STRONG AND
RESILIENT AND BRAVE AND JOYFUL.
LIKE ANY GARDEN OR WORK OF ART, IT HAD
TAKEN HER A LONG TIME TO MAKE
THINGS THE WAY THEY WERE. TO LEARN,
TO ARRANGE, TO REARRANGE.

Sometimes, she grew as much in one year as others do in five.

IT SHOWED. IN HER SPIRIT. IN HER LAUGH.
IT LOOKED AND IT SOUNDED LIKE WISDOM.
AND SHE LIKED IT THAT WAY.

"Things really changed,"
she said, "when I started to be
more generous to myself."

"I began to try to live like a tree," she said...

"WHO UNDERSTANDS THAT LIFE IS FILLED
WITH SEASONS AND EACH ONE HAS ITS WORTH.
I STOPPED FEARING THE LEAVES FALLING AWAY,
THE BARE BRANCHES. I UNDERSTOOD THAT SPRING
WOULD COME, THAT SUMMER WOULD COME,
THAT IT WAS ALL A PART OF MY LIVING."

She found that
the hot & the cold
could coexist.

SHE COULD HOLD SADNESS AND HOPE,
DISAPPOINTMENT AND JOY, FRUSTRATION
AND POTENTIAL AND HEARTACHE
ALL TOGETHER.

AND SHE SURPRISED HERSELF.
SHE DISCOVERED THAT SHE
DIDN'T BREAK. SHE DISCOVERED
SHE WAS MADE WITH AN
INCREDIBLE CAPACITY TO HOLD
ALL THAT LIFE IS MADE OF.

She found she was bigger
and more wonderful than
she had imagined.

"I won't apologize
for my contradictions,"
she said.

"A PHOTOGRAPH DOESN'T APOLOGIZE
FOR THE BLACKS, THE WHITES, THE
HUNDREDS OF GRAYS—IN THE END,
THEY MAKE THE PICTURE."

She went through life surprising herself. Finding hidden doors. Noticing the mysterious present. Seeing an old place as a place she'd never been.

"IN THIS WAY," SHE SAID, "I OPEN
MYSELF TO SEEING THE WORLD ANEW
AND SUDDENLY, I AM ASTONISHED
BY HOW BEAUTIFUL IT IS."

"Once," she said, "I stepped
outside of myself for a moment.

"I SAW MYSELF LIKE A STRANGER
ON THE STREET. I SAW WHAT OTHERS
LOVED IN ME—THE SUBSTANCE AND THE
SPARK THAT ARE MINE ALONE. AND I
REALIZED I OWED IT TO MYSELF TO SEE
THESE THINGS OFTEN. SO NOW I DO."

She realized that no one else's version of perfect would ever be right for her. So she made her own.

IT FIT HER BEAUTIFULLY. IT MOVED IN ALL
THE RIGHT PLACES. THERE WAS ROOM FOR LIGHT, AND
SPACE TO GROW, AND LOTS OF OPEN PLACES FOR
OPPORTUNITIES AND SPONTANEITY AND LITTLE GIFTS
THAT ONLY SHE WOULD RECOGNIZE.

"My priorities changed,"
she said, "I make time for
things that truly matter...

"OLD FRIENDS, FAVORITE BOOKS, GRAND
OPPORTUNITIES, GOOD CHOCOLATE, TINY
BEAUTIFUL THINGS. I ALWAYS WANTED MY LIFE
TO BE FILLED WITH ALL THAT I LOVED, AND
THEN I REALIZED IT WAS POSSIBLE. I JUST
HAD TO MAKE IT HAPPEN."

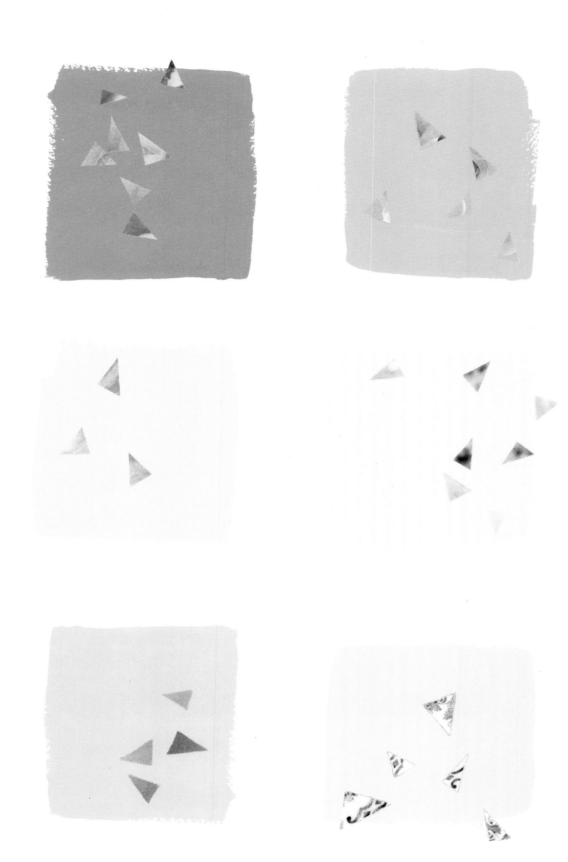

Some days, she wakes and the sun is shining through her windows

LIKE IT WANTS TO TALK SPECIALLY WITH HER,
AND SHE KNOWS THAT THIS IS GOING TO
BE A VERY GOOD DAY.

"Other days," she said, "there
may be only one wonderful moment.
I make it a point to appreciate it. And
usually, because I appreciated it, other
wonderful moments come along, just
to see what's happening."

*She made room in
every day for delight.*

She continued to believe
that the world was
very large and still full
of surprises.

She embraced a combination of hard work and magical thinking.

"YES," SHE SAID, "THE HARD WORK
MATTERS. BUT I ALWAYS LEAVE ROOM
FOR THINGS TO COME ALONG THAT
ARE EVEN BETTER THAN I COULD
HAVE PLANNED FOR."

She asked for the things she wanted. She invited them into the world.

*She cultivated
something she called
everyday courage.*

It meant believing that the world would catch her. It meant pushing the limits. It meant acting boldly. It meant she knew what she was worth.

———————

AND THE WORLD ALWAYS DID CATCH HER.
SOMETIMES THE LANDING WAS SOFT
AND SOMETIMES IT WAS NOT, BUT SHE ALWAYS
DISCOVERED IN THE END SHE WAS JUST
WHERE SHE NEEDED TO BE.

———————

She said fear meant only
one of two things:
don't do it, or do it anyway.

THE FIRST ONE FELT LIKE A
HAND HOLDING HER BACK, AND
THE SECOND FELT LIKE A HAND
PUSHING HER FORWARD.

She listened to her heart. As a voice of better reason.

AS A LITTLE GLOWING EMBER
THAT WANTED, LIKE THE NEEDLE OF
A COMPASS, TO LEAD HER TO THE
PLACE WHERE SHE SHOULD BE.

*She believed it was important
to know when the thing that
seems most wildly foolish is also
the thing that is perfectly right.*

She looked back and saw
that the rough times
had polished her.

She had challenges she could meet. She had friends who sustained her.

SHE HAD A COMPLETE AND
UNFAILING SENSE OF ALL
SHE WAS CAPABLE OF.

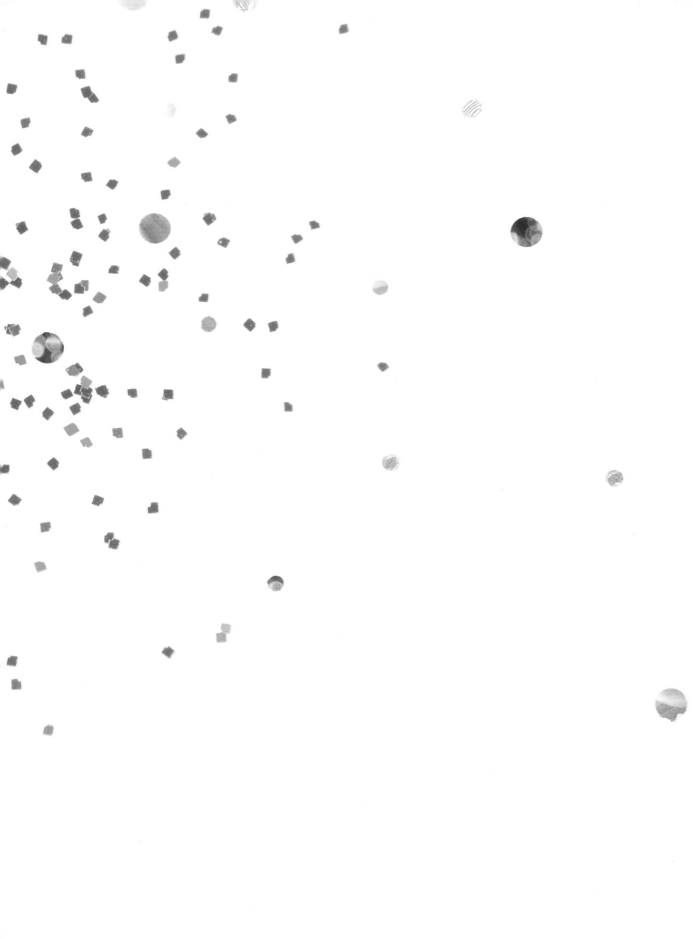

"At this very moment," she said,
"I am building a world so beautiful it is
always, even when it is complicated,
completely worth my while."

"Change is never easy,"
she said. "But I can
work with it.

———————

"BECAUSE CHANGE IS THE WORLD
MAKING ROOM FOR SOMETHING ELSE.
AND IT'S ENTIRELY POSSIBLE I'M
GOING TO REALLY LIKE IT."

———————

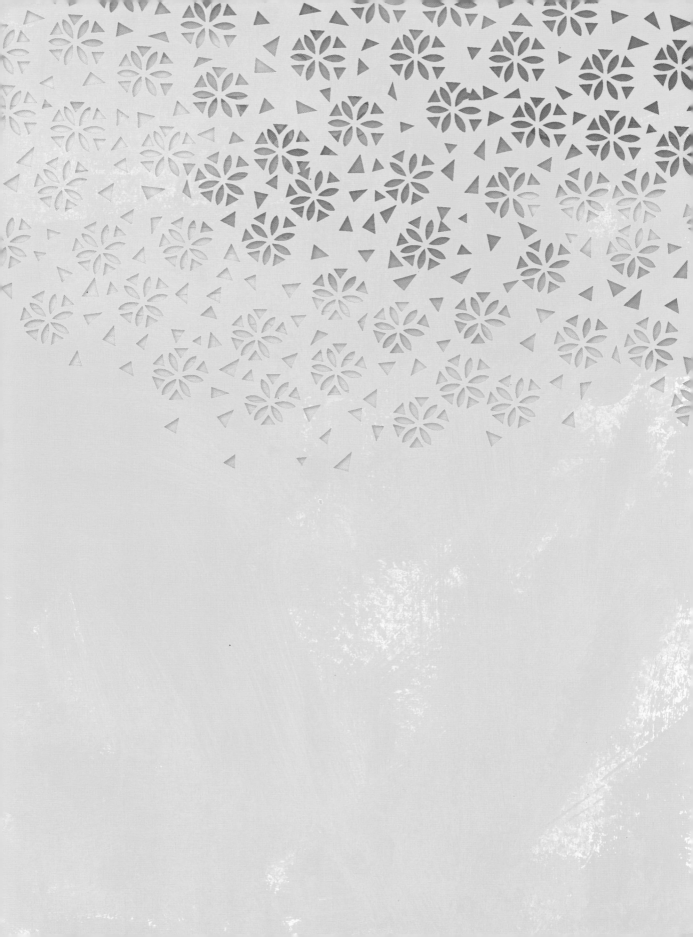

She created the
best possible
version of herself.

THE VERSION THAT
INCLUDED ALL OF HER.

———————————————

SHE PUT MORE LIFE
INTO HER LIFE.

"This," she said, "is a picture of me when I was still so young I had no idea of all the things that would be coming my way.

"I HAVE SUCH TENDERNESS FOR THAT WOMAN. I WANT TO SIT DOWN WITH HER AND TELL HER THAT THINGS ARE GOING TO BE MORE COMPLEX THAN SHE WILL EVER BE ABLE TO IMAGINE. AND MORE BEAUTIFUL, TOO. AND THAT SHE IS GOING TO TURN OUT OKAY."

She gave generously,
and she gave with joy.

BUT SHE ALWAYS SAVED
SOME OF HER FOR HERSELF.

She used to have a recurring dream

THAT THERE WAS SOMETHING BIG AND SERIOUS AND
SPECIFIC SHE NEEDED TO DO IN THE WORLD.

THEN, ONE DAY, SHE REALIZED
IT WASN'T A DREAM.

She had developed the ability to see the things that could be, hidden in the things that already were.

She narrowed the distance between the daydream and the day itself.

She decided she was not yet done with her transformation.

THERE WERE STILL INFINITE CITIES AND
COLORS AND CHANCES TO CONSIDER.

"I see," she said, "that my
life is a story of joy.

"I LOOK BACK AT THE HUGE, HIGH POINTS, THE SMALL, SATISFIED MOMENTS, THE DAYS THAT WERE FILLED WITH LOVE, AND SEE THAT THEY WERE EVERYWHERE RUNNING THROUGH THE FABRIC OF MY LIFE LIKE THREADS OF GOLD."

"It's true," she said,

"THERE MAY NEVER BE A PERFECT TIME,
SO I CHOOSE RIGHT NOW."

AND RIGHT NOW
CHOSE HER—COMPLETELY,
JOYFULLY—IN RETURN.

COMPENDIUM®

live inspired

With special thanks to the entire Compendium family.

CREDITS:

WRITTEN BY: M.H. CLARK

DESIGNED BY: JILL LABIENIEC

EDITED BY: AMELIA RIEDLER

CREATIVE DIRECTION BY: JULIE FLAHIFF

PHOTOGRAPHY CREDITS:

FRONT COVER: SIMONE BECCHETTI / STOCKSY.COM; PAGES 1, 70: LAMA-PHOTOGRAPHY / PHOTOCASE.COM; PAGES 5, 27: PENCAKE / PHOTOCASE.COM; PAGES 5, 27, 47: SALLY WALLIS / ISTOCK / THINKSTOCK; PAGES 7, 47: JALA / PHOTOCASE.COM; PAGES 8-9, 47: FANIEMAGE / PHOTOCASE.COM; PAGE 12: CLAUDIARNDT / PHOTOCASE.COM; PAGES 15, 19, 23, 27, 29, 33, 53, 57, 63: JILL LABIENIEC; PAGE 16: ADELE DE WITTE / ISTOCK / THINKSTOCK; PAGES 16, 27: SDANNAS / ISTOCK / THINKSTOCK; PAGES 16, 36: SÖR ALEX / PHOTOCASE.COM; PAGE 20: CHIORI / PHOTOCASE.COM; PAGES 24, 40, 41: GORTINCOIEL / PHOTOCASE.COM; PAGE 34: KIRSTEN SESSIONS; PAGES 34, 50, 61, 72: SEVERIJA / DOLLARPHOTOCLUB.COM; PAGE 36: JRB / DOLLARPHOTOCLUB.COM; PAGE 38: SHUWAL / LEUCHTSPUR.AT / PHOTOCASE.COM; PAGE 42: 3FORMAT / PHOTOCASE.COM; PAGE 45: DOROSBLACK / PHOTOCASE.COM; PAGE 48: TI.NA / PHOTOCASE.COM; PAGES 54, 68: BIT.IT / PHOTOCASE.COM; PAGE 58: FRANCESCA SCHELLHAAS / PHOTOCASE.COM; PAGE 60: BISGLEICH / PHOTOCASE.COM; PAGE 65: LMDB / PHOTOCASE.COM; PAGE 67: HOMYDESIGN / VEER.COM.

Library of Congress Control Number: 2014959336

ISBN: 978-1-938298-60-8

2nd printing. Printed in China with soy inks.